Confessions of a Banker

The Best Business Owners Buy Their Own Buildings

The How and Why to Blend Real
Estate With Your Business

Shane Mara

Copyright © 2024 Shane Mara
All rights reserved
First Edition

NEWMAN SPRINGS PUBLISHING
320 Broad Street
Red Bank, NJ 07701

First originally published by Newman Springs Publishing 2024

ISBN 978-1-63881-339-2 (Paperback)
ISBN 978-1-63881-340-8 (Digital)

Printed in the United States of America

This book is dedicated to my wife, who puts up with my entrepreneurial journey and who has stood beside me through all the ups and downs of that journey.

To my mom, Diane, and to my father who has passed, Jimmy, who taught me about character and hard work, those much-needed traits that are required to achieve any success in life.

To my kids, Jack and Alex, who are future leaders in the business world. They have watched up close and have seen my struggles and successes, and they are currently being trained daily to embark on their own business journeys.

To all my business owner friends and former clients, thank you for letting me enjoy the journey with you. Thanks for letting me see into your worlds of marrying the two dynamics of business and real estate together.

Contents

Introduction vii

My Story 1

1. Play Monopoly in Real Life....................7

2. Rent Never Increases 13

3. Debt Reduction 19

4. Appreciation of the Building 21

5. Cash Flow 27

6. Tax Benefits: Five Advantages............30

7. Increase Net Worth 33

8. Become More Bankable.......................38

9. Cushions Loss in the Event of Bankruptcy 43

10. Leverage 46

11. Perception 50

12. Being in Balance..............................54

13. First One Syndrome 57

14. How to Finance................................61

15. Partner with Investors 65

16. Due Diligence 73

17. Success Stories 75

Introduction

This book is written for all the everyday business owners out there, pursuing the real American Dream. Those brave few who have the desire to be great. Those who dare to create something out of nothing. The 5 percent. The ones who were told not to do it. Those who were told, "What you are doing is crazy," and who were told not to embark on that journey. Those who were told to just get a job and stay there till you retire, to play it safe. Those who were warned that it's not safe, that it's risky, that most businesses fail (which is true, by the way). Those who were told, "You can't do that. Don't do that. Please don't do that," by some (probably your parents).

Those brave few who dared to do the impossible and risk it all. To fly without the parachute. To get on the bull and ride it. To brave the cold and do what it takes. To not play it safe and to dare to dream. To have their own business, be their own boss, and not be told what to do.

The goal of every business owner is to do it right and be successful. To have a well-oiled machine that allows them to enjoy life to the fullest. To employ loads of people at great wages and make not only your dreams come true but the dreams of many more around you. To get to travel and see the world, all funded through the business. To build a long-term fortune that could be passed down from generation to generation. To be looked up to and revered in the community and have a platform. Ultimately, to make an impact. Sadly though, for so many (75%–95% of business owners), this never materializes.

Those dreams quickly turn into a nightmare. I too have had one of these businesses. I can remember those lonely, sleepless nights where you stare at the ceiling, wondering how you are going to survive. Wondering how you're going to make payroll on Friday. Wondering how you can make the bank's monthly payments. Wondering how you can pay your vendors, who will always make sure to call you regularly to get paid.

I remember on one—no, make that two occasions. I remember distinctly struggling to catch my breath, and I could not figure out why. But I quickly realized I was actually choking on anxiety and stress. Just writing about it makes me relive that painful moment. So I know what all the business owners out there are thinking and feeling. That is the unfortunate reality for most business owners. Most business owners are actually better off just having a J-O-B.

After living through that experience, I did come to the realization that working for the man is not such a bad thing. Having a secure paycheck every other

Friday, health care benefits, two- to three-week vacations, going home at five, and not having all the stress is actually quite enjoyable. I can tell you, there is absolutely no shame in doing that. If that is the case, do not feel like you have failed, because if you learn from your failures, which we all have plenty of, then nothing is a failure. It is always something we can learn and grow from, and as John Maxwell says, it becomes a launching pad for your success.

This book is written for the business owners out there, daring to dream the dream, hopefully putting forth the time, seeking the right counsel, and being successful. This book specifically is about adding a second income stream to your business. It is about buying your own building and, over the long term, having that become a huge part of the success of your business career.

I was a banker for fifteen years, and I can tell you, the most successful guys I knew married the successful business they had with commercial real estate—specifically, buying their own building for their business. That is what this book is about: not only *how* to buy your own building, but *why* you should buy your own building. I'm a big believer in understanding the *why*. In fact, the majority of this book focuses on the *why* and why it makes so much sense for not just a small portion of business owners but almost *all* of them.

If I could boil it down to one key secret of the majority of these business owners who are not just successful but are taking their success to another level, it was done when they started incorporating commercial real estate into their strategy of business. Quite a few of the guys became so good at it that they bought numerous properties, and unsurprisingly, the real estate component actually became far more valuable than the business itself.

You see, one of the key takeaways that we will mention over and over in this book is the fact that real estate becomes passive, and business is generally never passive. It is the opposite of passive, in that it is all-day, everyday work. It is the grind. Every business owner dreams of having a passive business, and I am telling you, one of the best ways for you to have that is to start buying commercial real estate for your business and grow from there.

My hope for this book is that you come to the same realization I have and that you will venture down the road of buying your own building and repeat that process multiple times in your tenure as a business owner.

Enjoy, and I hope to talk to you soon.

—Shane

My Story

One of the things I have really believed for a really long time is that everyone has a unique and fascinating story—the story of where they came from, the environment they grew up in, and a unique turning point, which altogether shaped who they are today. I, on the other hand, didn't think I had a very interesting story.

That changed when I was doing an interview for our podcast, and I shared what I thought was my boring story. Once it was over, it dawned on me that it was actually a pretty cool story. Then when the podcast was uploaded, I had a few friends reach out to me who told me how much they had enjoyed my story. I had one person who actually told me I needed to add this as a chapter in my book. Well, here it is.

I grew up in a rural West Texas town, in a middle-class family. My mom was one of eight children, and on my dad's side, he was one of four. I had a ton of cousins and aunts and uncles. We did not come from money. Money was always a struggle. On my dad's side of the family, no one had graduated college, and my mom's side only had a couple that graduated college.

My dad beat into me the idea that I was going to go to college and be the first one on his side of the family to do so. In fact, I never thought of anything less.

My dad's occupation growing up was that of a truck driver. I remember wanting to be like my dad. I remember telling him when I was a young child that I too wanted to drive a truck. His words in reply to me—and I still remember them—were "You will play hell." In our circle, that simply meant "There is no way in hell that you will be driving a truck when you get older."

He wanted me to be a banker. I wanted to be a truck driver. I didn't actually know what a banker was at the time. It's funny how life turns out. About twenty-five years later, I actually became a banker. He unfortunately never got to see that day.

My dad was actually very entrepreneurial. The business he started was his own trucking company. It was in the mid '80s, and if you know anything about Texas history from that time, you know that we had a massive oil bust. He specialized in moving oil rigs for the oil companies from site to site. Well, when the oil companies cannot pay you, you cannot pay anyone else. So that business unfortunately failed.

When a business fails, there are always damaging repercussions that people don't necessarily see, and we were no exception. My mom told me that he was owed $1 million by these oil companies, which he did not collect. So when he failed, he owed every bank in town.

During those times, filing bankruptcy was taboo. It was not like it is today. Today it is no big deal for companies to file for bankruptcy, but back then, it was a moral death sentence. Everyone in town saw you as a failure, and that left a huge scar on my dad.

I remember one time in my youth, having a police car show up at our house and a policeman knocked on the door to arrest my dad. I witnessed all this from my bedroom window. They actually came to arrest him for writing hot checks. I remember that at the time, as a young kid, I was devastated. My dad was my hero. He was my idol. And I remember seeing my idol being hauled away in the back of a police car.

The saddest part about that is, if he had been paid the money that was owed to him, things would've been radically different. In business though, recessions happen, downturns happen, and more times than not, the business owner loses everything.

After that, my dad got back into truck driving, but he was never happy. Hard to blame him, right? He muddled through driving a truck for several more years, but when you get a taste of being an entrepreneur, you always want to be an entrepreneur. So several years later, he resurrected with another business.

This time, he was given the franchise rights to a Massey Ferguson tractor dealership in a small neighboring town. He was back, baby. He was loving it again. This time, his parents, my grandparents, gave him a couple of acres of their land, which was on a major freeway, for him to build a building for the tractor dealership. So he built probably a 5,000 sq. ft building for the dealership.

This was in the early 1990s. If you know anything about Texas history, you also know that in the early '90s, we had another massive recession. This time, it wasn't just oil; it was overall. Long story short, my dad could not sell tractors because no one had any money. Unfortunately, a couple years after he opened, the dealership failed.

Once again, he filed bankruptcy, and he owed several banks in the town. When this happened, he was devastated not just physically, but mentally as an entrepreneur as well. When you fail as an entrepreneur, it is inevitable that you, the owner, will feel like a failure. You forget that 90 percent of all businesses fail in a ten-year period, and you internalize yourself as the only reason for the failure.

I can only imagine the amount of stress and anxiety my dad was feeling. Once again, he got back into truck driving, this time probably feeling more exasperated and hopeless than ever before.

As an older kid by that time, probably around the age of twenty, I had this image of business as something I wanted no part of. At that point, I was going to college and majoring in business, but I did not want anything to do with business itself. I was actually quite afraid of it.

I remember vividly that in my junior year of college, my dad went to the doctor and unexpectedly got the death sentence of cancer. He was gutted, as was the whole family. It was totally unexpected and horrific. He never went to the doctor to get checkups (some of that was obviously because of money), and unfortunately, when he finally went, they found giant golf ball-sized tumors in more than one place in his body. The time between when he was diagnosed and when he passed away was only three months. It was absolutely tragic.

I was trying to balance school and driving home on weekends to see him, and I almost quit. As you can imagine, it was one of the hardest times of my life, and even now, writing about this brings back some painful memories. But one of my distinct thoughts then was that the stress from running those two businesses was what had caused his demise. My thought was that I wanted nothing to do with business—ever.

My dad had partnered with my uncle on the tractor business, and one thing they did right was that they had built a building to house the dealership. They built about a 5,000 sq. ft building on my grandparents' property, which my grandparents had donated to my dad to start the business. So even though the business had failed, my mom and uncle still owned the building. They owed money to the bank, on a note, so to pay that note back, they rented out the building. They did not know anything about commercial real estate. They were a little out of pocket each month, so they did not have a great taste in their mouth about commercial real estate either. For them, it was an overall bad experience on the business side and on the real estate side.

Fast-forward about fifteen to eighteen months, and something really amazing happened. They listed the property for sale and found a buyer. The sales price was almost double of what they had built the property for. It was in the neighborhood of $225,000. At that moment, everything about how they felt about real estate changed. They went from hating it to loving it. I don't know the exact amount of money they netted out of that sale, but it was substantial. They had never had money of any significance in the bank prior to that sale. In an instant, their lives changed for the better.

For me, a real estate investor was born! My new philosophy became "I don't want anything to do with business, but I love real estate."

Play Monopoly in Real Life

Everyone absolutely loved the game of Monopoly as a child. The game was brought to light by Parker Brothers in 1935 and has sold over 275 million copies since its inception. Parker Brothers, which subsequently sold to Hasbro in 1991, has been selling this game since 1935, and year in and year out, it is one of their best-selling toys. I would care to venture the opinion that everyone reading this book knows how to play the game of Monopoly. It is a beloved favorite of businessmen everywhere.

The game of Monopoly is won by bankrupting all your opponents. I don't know about you, but my family and I have had several heated Monopoly games. At best, there would be some heated words, but at worst, a game board might be flipped on its head and someone would storm off in a fit. The reason was simple: if someone did a trade with another, we would all know the ramifications of that trade. Everyone would lose except the person who initiated the trade.

The initial target was always the youngest person in the family. We knew that, by sheer naivety, they might be willing to trade the missing invaluable property that was needed for the villain. After a few of those trades, even the youngest player in the family would know that any trade was a bad trade.

The game of Monopoly is won by getting hotels on certain properties. One of the things I find interesting about Monopoly is how it mirrors real life. In a game of Monopoly, getting a house on a property is a nice thing, as it is a form of income for you, but it will never win the game for you. What does win the game is getting a hotel, which, in reality, is nothing more than five houses on that one property.

Once you have this hotel, essentially five houses, you will win this game. Several times around the board, that crafty dog and dodgy top hat will start to go bankrupt. You will see other players start to drop one by one, until eventually, you are the victor.

How good is the sight of two or three shiny red hotels on your green/yellow/orange/baby blue properties? And getting to watch an opponent's facial expression and body language when they realize the dice have let them down is also quite a good feeling, I have to admit. Well, in real life, the best way to create wealth is to play the game of monopoly as well.

In real life, the best 401(k) plan is to buy a house, not in ones or twos, but in fives and tens and fifteens, just like in Monopoly. Then when you get these houses paid off, regardless of whether they go up in value or not, you will experience this beautiful thing called monthly residual cash flow. And that will be the greatest gift you will ever have financially.

It's all about cash flow, not just in business but personally as well. In our personal worlds, most of the individuals out there—let's say you and your family—probably need anywhere between $5,000 and $10,000 a month for your living expenses. That is the number we need to make monthly. Now if we want to retire, we still need to make a number that is close to this. I do understand that as we get older, we should have less of a monthly requirement, but for the sake of this conversation, let's keep these same numbers. I can also assure you that anyone reading this book wants to enjoy life and travel, especially in retirement, and that always costs a lot of money. In the road we are on, we have put too much work into creating wealth not to enjoy the fruit of that in our retirement. No one wants to retire like a pauper.

So the best way to cover this monthly requirement forever is to create a residual income stream that covers that. Now the proper purchase price for a rental property should be in the range of $100,000–$150,000, and the returns on that are easy to guesstimate. Here goes.

The first assumption is that you get these properties paid off (over a fifteen-year period). Let's say you have ten properties. The average property in that range should clear between $750 and $1,000 after all the expenses have been taken out (insurance, taxes, management fee, and maintenance costs). You multiply $1,000 by ten properties, and you have $10,000 residual income per month, which should easily cover your monthly expenditures.

If you have just one property, again it's nice, but you will only have about $1,000 coming in per month. That is not enough for you to retire, though it is a nice supplement. But we are talking about retiring properly, not adding supplements.

If you have five properties, your monthly income will be roughly $5,000 per month, assuming your properties are paid off. That should be enough to retire, but I would rather retire with a little enjoyment, for not much more effort.

What we have not included here are the appreciation figures. In real estate, you get to enjoy both cash flow and capital appreciation, and that is what makes this so attractive as an investment. Below is an example of what happens if you buy a $125,000 house and what the value is when the house is paid off, either in fifteen or twenty years. When you buy investment properties,

CONFESSIONS OF A BANKER

the bank generally allows one or the other as an amortization period.

$125,000	
2.5%	Value increase
Year 1	$128,125
Year 2	$131,328
Year 3	$134,611
Year 4	$137,977
Year 5	$141,426
Year 6	$144,962
Year 7	$148,586
Year 8	$152,300
Year 9	$156,108
Year 10	$160,011
Year 11	$164,011
Year 12	$168,111
Year 13	$172,314
Year 14	$176,622
Year 15	$181,037
Year 16	$185,563
Year 17	$190,202
Year 18	$194,957
Year 19	$199,831
Year 20	$204,827
Increase (%)	59.87%

In this scenario, in year 15, the house has risen in value to $181,037. The significance is, if you have ten houses that are now paid off, free and clear, then you are making $10,000 per month, and you have a net worth of this portfolio of houses at $1,810,370. You are essentially a multimillionaire by acquiring ten properties, just like in the game of Monopoly. It is without a doubt the best and easiest way to build the perfect retirement plan that combines cash flow *and* capital appreciation.

Now the reason I mention this in the very first chapter of the book, and especially about residential real estate when this whole book is about buying commercial real estate, is that I want you to have the right mindset about real estate in general. I am a fan of both residential and commercial, but residential is much easier to discuss in general, as well as in numbers and doing projections. In theory, commercial is similar; however, the numbers are much larger, and you do not need to buy as many properties. You might buy one commercial building at $1 million, which is the equivalent of our earlier example of eight residential properties at $125,000.

In summary, like the game of Monopoly, when you buy one house, it feels good, but you will not get rich off of one. It's nice, don't get me wrong, but you will not be able to retire off of one. You need multiples of fives and tens.

Now let's start playing Monopoly in real life.

Rent Never Increases

One of the most amazing attributes of owning your own building is unlike renting long-term, which have personal guarantees in them, but also have rental increases at a specified point in time, generally every year or every two years, sometimes less frequently.

So in a lease, you start out in year 1 and have rent much higher in year 5 and even higher in year 10. It's even higher in years 15 and 20. When you own your own building, the mortgage itself generally does not increase, because your rates are fixed. Sometimes the rates are fixed from three to five years, but some mortgages will be fixed for ten or fifteen years, with some even having twenty-year fixed rates. With every passing monthly payment and passing year, your balance goes down. It's a beautiful thing, and it is a huge selling point to buying a building.

So in year 20, your rent could be double what you started at in year 1. When you buy your own building and the banks put you on a twenty-year note, you have your building paid off, and you get a substantial rent reduction. Below is an example of a 2% yearly increase in rent.

2%	Increase
Year 1	$2,250
Year 2	$2,295
Year 3	$2,341
Year 4	$2,388
Year 5	$2,435
Year 6	$2,484
Year 7	$2,534
Year 8	$2,585
Year 9	$2,636
Year 10	$2,689
Year 11	$2,743
Year 12	$2,798
Year 13	$2,854
Year 14	$2,911
Year 15	$2,969
Year 16	$3,028
Year 17	$3,089
Year 18	$3,151
Year 19	$3,214
Year 20	$3,278
Total	$656,029
Increase (%)	45.68%

CONFESSIONS OF A BANKER

With a 2% increase yearly, you can see that at the twentieth year, rent has increased by 45.68%. The hardest part to wrap your head around is that you have spent over $650,000, and you have nothing to show for all the rent money you have spent. Here is the 3% yearly increase example.

3%	Increase
Year 1	$2,250
Year 2	$2,318
Year 3	$2,387
Year 4	$2,459
Year 5	$2,532
Year 6	$2,608
Year 7	$2,687
Year 8	$2,767
Year 9	$2,850
Year 10	$2,936
Year 11	$3,024
Year 12	$3,115
Year 13	$3,208
Year 14	$3,304
Year 15	$3,403
Year 16	$3,505
Year 17	$3,611
Year 18	$3,719
Year 19	$3,830
Year 20	$3,945
Total	$725,500
Increase (%)	75.35%

This looks even worse. Your rent has increased 75%, and you have paid over $725,000. And I remind you again, you have nothing to show for all this. *You are still renting!*

We have only looked at a marginal rent payment of $2,250. If you raise the rent payment to $5,000 as your starting payment, then check out this awful-looking twenty-year projection.

2%	Increase
Year 1	$5,000
Year 2	$5,100
Year 3	$5,202
Year 4	$5,306
Year 5	$5,412
Year 6	$5,520
Year 7	$5,631
Year 8	$5,743
Year 9	$5,858
Year 10	$5,975
Year 11	$6,095
Year 12	$6,217
Year 13	$6,341
Year 14	$6,468
Year 15	$6,597
Year 16	$6,729
Year 17	$6,864
Year 18	$7,001
Year 19	$7,141
Year 20	$7,284
Total	$1,457,842
Increase (%)	45.68%

We have the same amount of increase, 45.68%, but you have paid a total of over $1.4 million. And again, you have nothing to show for this. *You are still renting!* Look at how bad it is with a 3% increase.

3%	Increase
Year 1	$5,000
Year 2	$5,150
Year 3	$5,305
Year 4	$5,464
Year 5	$5,628
Year 6	$5,796
Year 7	$5,970
Year 8	$6,149
Year 9	$6,334
Year 10	$6,524
Year 11	$6,720
Year 12	$6,921
Year 13	$7,129
Year 14	$7,343
Year 15	$7,563
Year 16	$7,790
Year 17	$8,024
Year 18	$8,264
Year 19	$8,512
Year 20	$8,768
Total	$1,612,222
Increase (%)	75.35%

This is such a painful projection to look at. After twenty years, you have spent $1.6 million, and let me repeat, *you are still renting*!

What would this look like if you owned your building and were not renting? In this case, you would be looking at an amortization table, in which the figures go in the opposite direction, which is a refreshing and welcome sight versus the last four projections.

I cannot say enough about this. This is an incredible benefit to the business owner. Every business owner I know who has bought their own building has never regretted it. Generally, what they regret is that they did not buy it sooner in the day and that they had wasted rent for any of those years.

So why wait? Start today. Start looking for the property that suits your needs today.

Debt Reduction

One of the best things about owning real estate—and this includes commercial real estate as well—is the benefit of debt reduction. That reduction is a beautiful thing. Every month, you have a portion of your payment that covers interest, which is a tax write-off, but the other piece goes to reducing the debt. This is also what we call a forced savings account.

Over time, this forced savings account grows and grows. The ultimate goal for your commercial property is that, hopefully, in about fifteen years, you will have this property paid off.

I tell people this all the time when they are trying to calculate how much of an increase in value they'll get on their commercial real estate: just focus on getting the debt paid off. If you assume that it will not go up a penny in fifteen years but that you will get the debt paid off, you will still have an incredibly valuable asset that you owe nothing on.

At this point, you have a few options. You could rent out your building if you haven't already moved out. Two, you could refinance the building and pull the cash back out with no tax consequence. Three, you could just enjoy having no mortgage payment. And the last option is to sell the building and put that money in your own bank account.

In summary, whether or not the property goes up in value is not necessarily irrelevant, but it is less relevant than you would think. Your job as a business owner and as a real estate owner is to get the property paid off, free and clear. When you do, all kinds of options open up to you.

Now if you enjoy a time of extreme appreciation, your opportunities really open up. You could use that additional equity for a refinance or do a line of credit for your business, which we will talk about at great length later on in the book.

Appreciation of the Building

Historically, real estate appreciates anywhere between 2% and 5%. That obviously can vary based on location and economic conditions. I live in Texas, and we have had various economic cycles to deal with over the last forty to fifty years. We had an oil bust in the mid '80s, which caused commercial real estate to decline. We experienced the S&L collapse in the early '90s, which saw commercial buildings drop massively in value. In 2008, we also saw commercial values drop, although they did not drop as significantly as most would think. The prices stayed relatively firm during that time.

Outside of those events, real estate and commercial real estate have risen in price substantially. If you average out all the historical cycles, then commercial real estate would fall into that same range of 2%–5% yearly increases.

Appreciation is very real, and based on historical representation, it is something you can probably count on to continue going forward. The simple reason is that there are a lot of small businesses out there, and a lion's share of them need a building to operate.

When this occurs, it really adds to the increase in your net worth. Let's say you buy a building for $500,000. In fifteen years, you could potentially have the building paid off, and the building could be worth $1 million by then. That would mean that you'd have doubled your money from your purchase price. This happens in so many cases. You can't say all of them, but I would say this happens in the majority of cases. Even if you bought at the peak and sold in the low of a recession, I would argue that you would still make money. *But* you would most likely have all or a large portion of the building paid off, and you would still have created a valuable part of your net worth.

This is why real estate has created more millionaires over time than any other industry. I do not see that changing anytime soon. The population continues to increase, business openings seem to increase, and demand therefore increases.

Appreciation is the cream. It's the gravy. It is the icing on the cake. In theory, you do not even need appreciation for the building to still make so much sense; however, appreciation will happen, and it will more than likely be larger than you expected over a long period.

The majority of you reading this book have owned your homes for probably a considerable length of time, so you know that appreciation is very real, as I would imagine that almost all of you guys have experienced it. So don't fight it; just accept that it is more than likely going to happen. Below is a chart of two scenarios of appreciation, one at 2.5% and one at 5%, on a purchase price of $750,000.

2.5%	Value increase
Year 1	$750,000
Year 2	$768,750
Year 3	$787,969
Year 4	$807,668
Year 5	$827,860
Year 6	$848,556
Year 7	$869,770
Year 8	$891,514
Year 9	$913,802
Year 10	$936,647
Year 11	$960,063
Year 12	$984,065
Year 13	$1,008,667
Year 14	$1,033,883
Year 15	$1,059,730
Year 16	$1,086,224
Year 17	$1,113,379
Year 18	$1,141,214
Year 19	$1,169,744
Year 20	$1,198,988
Increase (%)	59.87%

In the first scenario, at 2.5%, you can see the massive increase in values. You will find out quickly enough that most of the commercial banks will only give you a max term of twenty years. So in this scenario, you will have your building paid off, and it will be worth $1.2 million. That is only a 60% increase. You would assume that you could probably do better than that, but who would not take that?

Also, most banks require you to put a 20% down payment when you buy a commercial building, so in this scenario, they would have made you put $150,000 down. So in this scenario, you actually increased your money from a $150,000 investment to $1.2 million. That is an increase of $1.05 million.

That is an increase of 699%! That is the beauty of what we are talking about here, the leverage you are getting. You are not just getting a 60% increase, but you are getting a 699% increase. I ask again, who wouldn't take that?

Initial down	$150,000
Value in year 20	$1,198,988
Increase of 699.33%	$1,048,988

Sometimes we struggle with understanding a return that large. Once it gets over 100%, we lose context. So I like to think in terms of doubling your money (from $150,000), or doubles. In this scenario, you doubled your money at $300,000 (1), then again at $450,000 (2), then at $600,000 (3), then at $750,000 (4), then at $900,000 (5), then at $1.05 million (6), then lastly, at $1.2 million (7). That's seven doubles. That's incredible, but look at our returns at 5% yearly.

5%	Value increase
Year 1	$750,000
Year 2	$787,500
Year 3	$826,875
Year 4	$868,219
Year 5	$911,630
Year 6	$957,211
Year 7	$1,005,072
Year 8	$1,055,325
Year 9	$1,108,092
Year 10	$1,163,496
Year 11	$1,221,671
Year 12	$1,282,755
Year 13	$1,346,892
Year 14	$1,414,237
Year 15	$1,484,949
Year 16	$1,559,196
Year 17	$1,637,156
Year 18	$1,719,014
Year 19	$1,804,964
Year 20	$1,895,213
Increase (%)	152.70%

Look at this one, as it is so much better. In this scenario, you have increased your investment by 152.70%. You originally bought the building for $750,000, and it is now worth $1.9 million. In that same twenty-year period, you paid this building off completely. The bank calls that "paid in full." But don't forget your cash-on-cash return; that is the real return. You invested $150,000 of your own cash, and it is now worth $1.9 million.

Initial down	$150,000
Value in year 20	$1,895,213
Increase of 1163.48%	$1,745,213

This one is really tough to grasp. In this scenario, you doubled your money at $300,000 (1), then again at $450,000 (2), then at $600,000 (3), then at $750,000 (4), then at $900,000 (5), then at $1.05 million (6), then at $1.2 million (7), then at $1.35 million (8), then at $1.5 million (9), then at $1.65 million (10), then at $1.8 million (11). That's eleven doubles. That's even more incredible. That is why we love real estate, but more importantly, that is why we must buy our own building.

Our business has to have a place to reside, and why throw that money away to a landlord and not back in our own pockets? This is one of the strongest reasons that I advocate for business owners to buy their own buildings. These numbers are real, and they are very doable and too incredible to ignore.

I beg of you to buy your own building.

Cash Flow

Cash flow is everything to a business, so when we are talking about buying a building, we cannot have too much of a cash flow burn monthly. Now we know that we have to come up with the down payment. For the majority of people reading this book, that may be a problem, which we will address in its own chapter, but we have to maintain a similar monthly mortgage payment to our rent payment.

My advice for all of you business owners is to buy a building that has additional space for you to rent out. In the commercial space, we call that multitenant. In some instances, you will need all the space, but do not get hung up on that. It just has to make sense for you for now.

The goal with a multitenant is that your mortgage payment will actually go down or remain flat in cost. That is the ideal scenario. That does not always have to be the case, as a lot of times, you might pay more to own your own building, but hopefully, other variables outweigh that additional cost. For instance, I had a friend/client who was officing out of 2,000 sq. ft, but he needed to increase that to about 5,000 sq. ft.

That additional cost was going to more than double his payment.

He found a building that had over 7,000 sq. ft, which he bought for just north of $500,000, and his payment ended up being about $2,000 less than what the new rent would have been. I interviewed him about six months after the purchase, and he was so happy he had made the decision to buy. One of his answers is exactly what I hope all of you will say: "I'm ready to buy the next one."

I can tell you that that business owner has been looking for the next one for quite some time now. He is specifically looking for a multitenant building with his goal of paying no rent at all for his business, with the monthly mortgage being covered by the other tenants.

If you can create the multitenant situation, then that is the most ideal situation you can be in when it comes to owning your own building, as the rental income will be important for your own cash flow.

One question you might have is, how much of an increase is too much for the new mortgage payment? That is a question of how much excess cash flow you currently have. If you already pay rent, then you know you can or have been at least covering that amount. Now the payment is going to be the total of the monthly mortgage payment, insurance, taxes, and maintenance (just like your primary residence). Take that amount and subtract that from your current rent, and that is the excess you will be responsible for covering. The first

CONFESSIONS OF A BANKER

question is, can your business support that monthly increase?

This is where I will make the plug to make sure you input your monthly figures into some kind of accounting system, like QuickBooks. It is imperative that you know your numbers. I am sure you have heard that if you can't measure your business, then you really cannot manage your business. I am a big fan of building KPIs (key performance indicators) into one's financial model. Those are the essential measures of your business. It is, in a nutshell, how your business performs in a few major key metrics. You have got to do this. It is a must.

Once you have those figures, you can easily determine if you can afford this new added cost to your business. If you have any doubts, I would not proceed until you have that confidence supported by the financials.

Tax Benefits
Five Advantages

Now for the tax benefits. This is generally what a large portion of business owners gloss over and tune out. Just like the rest of the book, I am going to keep this short and sweet. Make sure you always consult a tax professional before finalizing your decision, but just know that this investment can be a tax benefit-rich asset.

Interest expense

The first benefit we are going to discuss is the interest portion of the mortgage payment. Each payment is broken down into two parts, principal and interest. The interest portion is tax-deductible.

Depreciation expense

The premise of depreciation is simply the wearing down of the building or the structure of the property. You cannot depreciate land, because it simply does not wear down over time and generally appreciates. Currently, depreciation on commercial buildings is done over a 39-year period, and residential buildings over a 27.5-year period. For instance, if an investor purchases a $1 million commercial building and the building value is $800,000, they can take approximately $20,512 ($800,000 divided by 39) of depreciation each year.

Non-mortgage deductions

Renovations, maintenance, other ongoing improvements, and other expenses related to owning a commercial property are also potential deductions. These are out-of-pocket expenses you can deduct every year, but so many of these improve the value of your building.

Capital gains

When you sell a property for more than you originally purchased it for, the profit will be taxed as a short-term or long-term capital gain, which is typically a lower tax rate than ordinary income tax.

Short-term capital gains, properties held for less than one year, can range from 10% to 39% depending on your income bracket. Long-term capital gains, which are properties held for a year and one day or more, are taxed at much more favorable rates, ranging from 0% to 20% depending on your tax bracket.

1031 tax-deferred exchanges

The 1031 exchange is another tool that business owners can utilize to their benefit. A 1031 exchange allows business owners to defer the payment of capital gains taxes as long as they exchange their property for another "like-kind" commercial property within a certain period. This like-kind property must be of greater or equal value to the selling property and cannot be a home used as their personal residence.

However, the 1031 exchange does not allow an investor to defer their capital gains indefinitely; at some point, when the new property is sold, the business owner will have to pay their taxes in full. But there is no limit to how many times the business owner can buy and sell property inside the 1031 exchange umbrella.

Beyond taxes, a business owner buying his own building sometimes serves as a de facto succession plan. Since many businesses do not have solid succession plans in place, the investment in a building can mean that a company has a guaranteed asset at the end of its life, even if there isn't someone who wants to carry on running the business.

Increase Net Worth

We have gone in depth about how buildings appreciate over time and how the principal reduction affects your equity. In general, a building will increase your net worth over time. Combine that with the leverage of buying multiple properties, and this will greatly compound your net worth.

When people start a business, everyone has grand visions of making a lot of money and employing a lot of people, but everyone unanimously wants to have a great lifestyle. This great lifestyle means having the freedom to travel, buying a nice home, buying nice cars, and enjoying all the fruit of that hard work. It means security not just for today but in the long term. One of the real problems with owning a business is that it is very difficult for that business to ever be *passive*.

Real estate is passive by nature. That is the real beauty of this asset class. If I had my choice of building a real estate empire or a business empire, I would build a real estate empire every time. The reason is that, over time, real estate gives you lifestyle.

Once it is built and all the hard work has been done, meaning that the buildings have been paid off, you don't really have to do anything other than go to the mailbox, unlike a business, which the business owner will generally have to think about and worry about nonstop. We talked about how 75%–95% of small businesses fail over a ten-year period, but if you take the ones that actually succeeded, I would bet that 80% of those businesses are not passive by nature. I would bet that the business owners are there thirty to forty hours a week to ensure the success and fluency of the business.

When you contrast that with the successful real estate investors who have had their properties paid off, these guys might work two to five hours a week. One of the hard parts of their life is figuring out what vacation they want to take next or what they want to do over the weekend. These are completely different lifestyles.

This is what is so great about the small business owner buying his own building—the increase in net worth. A business owner can sell the business and then rent out the building to the new buyer. They can actually make that part of the sale a potential leaseback for five, ten, fifteen, or even twenty years. This will create a cash flow for that period.

In this scenario, you have swapped an active lifestyle for a passive lifestyle. This is the true reason business owners get into business! You want the ability to live a comfortable lifestyle and at the same time have the flexibility, not the anxiety, that comes with being an entrepreneur. This is the real reason you have become an entrepreneur. This is also the reason you want to own your own building.

CONFESSIONS OF A BANKER

Below is the same chart we used in a previous chapter, which shows what your net worth is going to be after paying off your building.

	$1,000,000	$800,000	**$200,000**	20.0%
3.0%	Value increase	Balance	**Equity**	Equity (%)
Year 1	$1,030,000	$776,102	**$253,898**	24.7%
Year 2	$1,060,900	$750,980	**$309,920**	29.2%
Year 3	$1,092,727	$724,574	**$368,153**	33.7%
Year 4	$1,125,509	$696,816	**$428,692**	38.1%
Year 5	$1,159,274	$667,639	**$491,635**	42.4%
Year 6	$1,194,052	$636,969	**$557,084**	46.7%
Year 7	$1,229,874	$604,729	**$625,145**	50.8%
Year 8	$1,266,770	$570,840	**$695,930**	54.9%
Year 9	$1,304,773	$535,217	**$769,556**	59.0%
Year 10	$1,343,916	$497,772	**$846,144**	63.0%
Year 11	$1,384,234	$458,411	**$925,823**	66.9%
Year 12	$1,425,761	$417,036	**$1,008,725**	70.7%
Year 13	$1,468,534	$373,545	**$1,094,989**	74.6%
Year 14	$1,512,590	$327,828	**$1,184,762**	78.3%
Year 15	$1,557,967	$279,772	**$1,278,195**	82.0%
Year 16	$1,604,706	$229,258	**$1,375,449**	85.7%
Year 17	$1,652,848	$176,159	**$1,476,689**	89.3%
Year 18	$1,702,433	$120,344	**$1,582,089**	92.9%
Year 19	$1,753,506	$61,673	**$1,691,833**	96.5%
Year 20	$1,806,111	$0	**$1,806,111**	100.0%

This shows what will happen if you buy a building for $1,000,000 with $200,000 as down payment. In twenty years, your net worth will go up to $1,806,111 on 3% annual increases. Your net worth in that example truly goes from $200,000 to $1,806,111.

You have to keep in mind that your net worth at the time of the purchase is only the amount of money you put down. You double your money at $400,000; $600,000; $800,000; $1 million; $1.2 million; $1.4 million; $1.6 million; and finally, $1.8 million. That is eight doubles over the course of a twenty-year period. That is truly amazing.

Over the years, as a banker, I have had numerous clients who, after they bought the first property, bought a second property and a third property and a fourth property. You have to keep in mind that these assumptions are based on you at least renting your property for the amount that is owed each month. Keep in mind, your goal with these properties is not just to break even from the standpoint of rent versus your debt obligations; your goal is to also enjoy cash flow along the way.

If you were to buy a second building that cost $1 million and you did the same thing for a twenty-year period, you would have a net worth of almost $4 million.

There's a big difference between commercial tenants and residential tenants. What I like about commercial tenants is that they derive their livelihood from that commercial business. I would rather have that type of tenant than a residential tenant.

The laws also favor residential tenants versus commercial tenants. In the commercial world, if they don't pay, you can simply lock the door and keep all their contents. You also get an individual guarantee from the business owner.

The leases are also long-term leases and not six months to one year. So although the leases are harder to get, once you get a commercial tenant, it is much more favorable.

Become More Bankable

As I mentioned before, I have worked for a bank for fifteen years, and one of the fascinating things about banking is which loans the banks actually prefer. There is one loan in particular that banks line up to do. They give you the best rates and the best terms. They fight for the business. They will offer rates that they normally don't offer. They will allow you to put smaller down payment amounts than they would allow otherwise. That loan is the owner-occupied commercial real estate loan.

If you will allow me to go into a little bit of detail about banking here. Here are some of the categories of bank loans: commercial real estate, residential real estate, car loans, home improvement loans, equipment loans, accounts receivable loans, lines of credit, etc. In the banking world, each one of these categories has lending limits attached to it. In short, a bank can only lend so much in each category, and that threshold is determined by the Federal Reserve.

In the banking world, we would call these buckets, and we could never be over the limit in any of these categories. Now there is one loan out there that is so good that it is not a part of these ratios. This means you can lend as much as you want without any repercussions from the Fed. That loan is the owner-occupied commercial real estate loan.

Now banking has been around a really long time, and historically, this has been the best-performing loan category, period. You can see why. The owner of a business derives his livelihood from his business. He also has to operate his business at a certain location. You marry those two together, and it becomes a very important place for this business owner.

He has a vested interest in his business succeeding, and consequently, he has a vested interest in the building succeeding as well. You combine that, along with the historical appreciation of real estate in general and the reduction of debt from the monthly payment the owner is required to pay, and you have the perfect loan. The default rate in this category is incredibly low, and of course, the banks and the Federal Reserve know this. That is why they both clamor for this type of loan.

This loan *does not* count against the ratios of a bank. That means they can lend as much as they want in this bucket. There is no limit, and that is why they love this category so much. In summary, lending has gotten very tough over the years, but the one loan that banks absolutely want to do is the one loan that all of you business owners reading this book need to run out and buy.

When you go from a building that you rent to a building that you own, you become more *bankable* in the eyes of the bank. You actually go up a level in their eyes. What you will find is, they will become more willing to allow you access to capital, which is one of the critical factors of growth for a company.

One of the main reasons is that they know every one of the attributes written about in this book is correct. They know that you're going to increase the business's net worth. They know about the depreciation benefits. They know about the appreciation of the building. They know about your rent never increasing. The bottom line is, your business is now more valuable to the bank than it was before.

Now the banks will generally make you put 20% down on the loan (sometimes less), so you and the bank have that piece in equity right out of the gate. But on a twenty-year note, after paying on the note for two years, you now have 30% equity on the building, on a 3% value increase. You are at almost 40% equity after four years, so you can see how quickly you build equity in these buildings.

Below is a chart of what I am talking about with a $1 million building that a buyer puts 20% down on.

	$1,000,000	$800,000	**$200,000**	20.0%
3.0%	Value increase	Balance	**Equity**	Equity (%)
Year 1	$1,030,000	$776,102	**$253,898**	24.7%
Year 2	$1,060,900	$750,980	**$309,920**	29.2%
Year 3	$1,092,727	$724,574	**$368,153**	33.7%
Year 4	$1,125,509	$696,816	**$428,692**	38.1%
Year 5	$1,159,274	$667,639	**$491,635**	42.4%
Year 6	$1,194,052	$636,969	**$557,084**	46.7%
Year 7	$1,229,874	$604,729	**$625,145**	50.8%
Year 8	$1,266,770	$570,840	**$695,930**	54.9%
Year 9	$1,304,773	$535,217	**$769,556**	59.0%
Year 10	$1,343,916	$497,772	**$846,144**	63.0%
Year 11	$1,384,234	$458,411	**$925,823**	66.9%
Year 12	$1,425,761	$417,036	**$1,008,725**	70.7%
Year 13	$1,468,534	$373,545	**$1,094,989**	74.6%
Year 14	$1,512,590	$327,828	**$1,184,762**	78.3%
Year 15	$1,557,967	$279,772	**$1,278,195**	82.0%
Year 16	$1,604,706	$229,258	**$1,375,449**	85.7%
Year 17	$1,652,848	$176,159	**$1,476,689**	89.3%
Year 18	$1,702,433	$120,344	**$1,582,089**	92.9%
Year 19	$1,753,506	$61,673	**$1,691,833**	96.5%
Year 20	$1,806,111	$0	**$1,806,111**	100.0%

You can see from the equity above how fast it builds and why the bank would be willing to give you more capital. They can always attach anything negative to the equity of the building. Consequently, at some point in time, it would also give the appearance that the bank would actually like for you to fail because they would have so much equity in your building.

A logical business owner would think that, but in reality, most banks would rather that you just continue to pay the mortgage payment. The reason is that past-due loans are viewed so negatively inside the banking industry. The Fed views them negatively, and if a bank tries to foreclose on a customer who has substantial equity, then the Fed will look into the factors as to why the business owner wouldn't have sold the building versus letting the bank have it back. The risk is not worth the reward in the bank's eyes.

Consequently, one of the hardest loan types to get in the banking industry is a line of credit. But as the equity in your building starts to increase, the bank will gladly let you tap into some of that equity in the form of a line of credit. A line of credit for your business is one of the most important loans you can get.

Becoming more bankable is something that is rarely talked about in the business and banking world, but it is very real.

Cushions Loss in the Event of Bankruptcy

This is absolutely something that no one wants to talk about. The sad reality is that about 75%–95% of all small businesses fail over the course of about ten years. That number comes from research from different countries over different time spans.

What I always hate are the tragic consequences of a business on the brink of bankruptcy; generally, you have an individual losing his life savings, a lot of times getting a divorce, getting health issues from the stress, or having strained relationships with their sons and daughters. Those are things no one ever talks about when you see a business fail. This absolutely breaks my heart. This is why I do what I do and why I am writing this book.

If your business has been open for longer than two years from the time you owned your building, my bet is that you have quite a bit of equity in your building. Because of the large down payment, two years of principal, and the appreciation, you should have substantial equity.

From our previous chapter, using the example of the building that had a purchase price of $750,000, with an appreciation rate of 2.5%, in two years you will have equity of $231,828, and then $343,428 after five years. That large amount of equity will cushion your losses in the event of bankruptcy, and those numbers grow substantially every passing year you remain in business.

	$750,000	$600,000	
2.5%	Value increase	Balance	**Equity**
Year 1	$768,750	$583,049	**$185,701**
Year 2	$787,969	$556,141	**$231,828**
Year 3	$807,668	$546,224	**$261,444**
Year 4	$827,860	$526,240	**$301,620**
Year 5	$848,556	$505,128	**$343,428**
Year 6	$869,770	$482,826	**$386,944**
Year 7	$891,514	$459,265	**$432,249**
Year 8	$913,802	$434,376	**$479,426**
Year 9	$936,647	$408,082	**$528,565**
Year 10	$960,063	$380,306	**$579,757**
Year 11	$984,065	$350,963	**$633,102**
Year 12	$1,008,667	$319,964	**$688,703**
Year 13	$1,033,883	$287,217	**$746,666**
Year 14	$1,059,730	$252,622	**$807,108**
Year 15	$1,086,224	$216,077	**$870,147**
Year 16	$1,113,379	$177,469	**$935,910**
Year 17	$1,141,214	$136,684	**$1,004,530**
Year 18	$1,169,744	$93,599	**$1,076,145**
Year 19	$1,198,988	$48,083	**$1,150,905**
Year 20	$1,228,962	$0	**$1,228,962**
Increase (%)	59.87%		

Now that is something no one wants to talk about, but not only is the equity fairly easy to access with the bank in the form of a line of credit, it is also your backstop as a business owner if things get really difficult for your business.

Contrast that with the business owner who has three years remaining on a lease and who is filing for bankruptcy. Those landlords get nasty when you do not fulfill your obligations—in this case, fulfill the entirety of the lease.

These guys will come after you with attorneys. They will get judgments. It is just a business decision for these guys, and they are well versed in suing you after the fact. So when you're going through the hardest time of your life, it is compounded by these individuals trying to inflict even more harm on you. It is a horrible place to be, I can promise you that.

In the worst-case scenario in which this happens, you will hate to lose your building and the equity, but you will be very grateful when all these debtors do not come after you because you had some equity in your building.

Leverage

Leverage, as defined by *Merriam-Webster*, is "the use of credit to enhance one's speculative capacity."

While that is true, what I love about real estate is that individuals or businesses have to have places to live and operate. The demographics just continue to support increased population, which means more individuals and businesses. So just the simple law of supply and demand is in our favor as far as leverage goes; more people need more housing and more commercial real estate. In this chapter, we are going to go over the real benefits of leverage.

It *is* one of the greatest benefits of real estate. It is the ability to put a fraction of the total cost down on a property (5%–20%) and still be able to buy the property and have a third party, which in most cases is a bank, finance the remainder.

This particular asset class (owner-occupied real estate), as we will go over later on in this book, is so powerful because the bank is willing to let you put the least amount down in this scenario. SBA will allow you as little as 5%–10%, while commercial banks will generally allow 20% down. I worked for a bank for many years, and I can tell you, this asset class was our favorite one. So take advantage of that.

When a business owner buys a building that costs $800,000, he only has to come up with anywhere between $80,000 and $160,000. I know that for so many business owners, that is still a huge chunk of capital to part with, or they just don't have it in general; however, that is a fantastic figure.

I tell so many real estate investors or potential real estate investors that where there is a will, there is a way. This is especially true when it comes to the down payment of your first commercial building as a business owner. My advice is, if you don't have it, *figure it out*. Where there is a will, there is a way. You can always partner with other investors. We will go over this in more detail in the chapter called "Partnering with Investors."

Another form of leverage is used when you have owned your commercial building for a lengthy period, and you now have substantial equity through paying down the debt and capital appreciation. The banks will then potentially allow you to buy a second building and use this equity as your down payment.

Now on your second building, you will owe 100% of the acquisition price because you have essentially put *no* money down. While that will make for a substantial increase in the monthly payment, it will also allow you to leverage a second building with no money out of your pocket. The hope is that your business has grown, and you now need this extra space. Or a really good deal has landed in your lap, and you want to take advantage of it.

Also, at this point, you are going to have to decide what you are going to do with your first building. You can keep building 1 and hopefully rent it out and let the tenant pay off your mortgage. You can then enjoy the beauty of debt reduction and capital appreciation on someone else's dime (the tenant). *That is the essence of the entire book, by the way. This is the real secret to wealth.*

You could also sell your building. At that point, the bank is going to want a certain portion for the down payment of the second building, which you did not put down upon its acquisition. But if you do sell, you should have substantial capital from the proceeds.

For me, the determining factor is *the amount of capital you have in the bank*. If you are low on funds, then you might need to sell building 1. If you feel like you have a substantial amount of capital, then I would keep the building and rent it out. But I say this all the time: there is no wrong answer between those two options.

You may look back ten years later and wish you had never sold that building, but what did you do with the money when you sold building 1? Did it help you buy a third building? Did it help you expand your business, and did that drive increased revenue for the next ten years? Did you buy a lake house and see that appreciate and get paid off? You'll have to weigh that out, but in the moment, you did what you thought was right.

You could also leverage that equity in other forms as well. You could get a cash loan for other ventures (lines of credit, a vacation home, the purchase of another business, etc.). But leveraging real estate, with paying down debt over time and enjoying capital appreciation, is the real reason this asset class has created more millionaires than any other.

Perception

This is one of my favorite attributes. When you buy your own building, the perceptions of four people change dramatically—your customers, your competitors, your bank, and most importantly, *you*.

The perception of your customers/vendors and how they view your business goes up. Depending on the type of business, some of your customers/vendors may not know you have bought your own building, but don't be afraid to brag on yourself for this one. Have an open house to showcase the new digs. Think of a reason to invite your top ten vendors or customers to your new facility. Shoot a high-quality video with your workers doing something fun and post it on your website and social media. When your vendors/customers see these, they will think differently about your business. You elevate a level in their mind.

Your competitors will think differently when they come to that conclusion as well. They will watch the same video you posted on social media. They will wonder what you are doing to be so successful. They will be curious to know if you are doing anything differently than they are doing. If they didn't feel you

CONFESSIONS OF A BANKER

were that much of a threat before, they will now. You may never hear the words, but the perception of your business will grow in the eyes of your competitors.

Your bank as well will have a different level of respect and admiration for your business. All loans and capital that you want to acquire from this time forward will be easier to get. The reason is simple: the equity in your building will potentially cover any additional loan loss going forward. Bankers from other banks will come out of the woodwork to find you. They will be researching owners of buildings in certain areas, and you/your business will show as the owner. You will then be getting all the annoying solicitation calls, and not just from bankers wanting to do business with you.

This also can be a real opportunity, as you might be able to get a much-reduced rate or better terms on your loan. If your bank becomes too conservative, you can now use the building to obtain loans that your bank may not want to do, but that another bank might be more than willing to do. This can be used to acquire a second building or some other investment you want to do. But make no mistake, the building lays the foundation for all opportunities in the future.

Your new perspective of your business equals confidence. Confidence, whether in life or business, is sometimes fleeting. Sometimes you have a great deal of it, and other times, you struggle to have any of it. I can tell you that, as a business owner, you almost need confidence like you need to breathe, as it is very important to your business.

I firmly believe you do not want to be arrogant; you want to be humble, as that helps keep your mind open for new ideas and new ways to improve your business. But you do need confidence. It is very difficult to grow if you are arrogant, because more times than not, you are close-minded to fresh ideas; you believe that you already have the best way of doing things.

This has an amazing knock-on effect for you and your business. In my opinion though, the biggest benefactor is you, the business owner. I am a huge believer in personal development and being consistent in that endeavor. Just trying to do an extra 1 percent per day over a long period turns into massive increases. Whether a business owner believes in this or not, when you buy your own building, your acumen increases.

That difficult process of acquiring and stabilizing your own commercial property not only grows your acumen, but the perception of your business also grows immensely. This has a hidden effect on your business. Again, it is very difficult to quantify, but it is very real.

A lot of work goes into the purchase of a building—a lot of time spent looking at different properties, effort in obtaining all the proper documentation for the banks, and research in due diligence of the property and maybe zoning/rezoning requirements. Generally, no building is absolutely perfect and ready to move into. The building renovation can quite often be a massive undertaking. While this process is substantial, all this work only increases the skill level of the business owner.

This newfound skill level is the foundation for a new future in commercial real estate, which, if tapped into, could lead to your next business and almost certainly part of your retirement. I said earlier that of all the successful business owners who had gone before that bought that first building, which led to a second and a third and so on and so on, the most successful business owners I knew married these two worlds together. It all starts with the skill acquired in acquiring the first property.

Being in Balance

This is a chapter I almost didn't put in the book, because it doesn't necessarily relate to buying a building; it relates more to the overall health and satisfaction of the business owner. I did want to put this in the book because I am such a firm believer in small-business owners having a great balance between work and the rest of their life.

I am called to help business owners in all areas of business. In the circles I have had the privilege to run in, I see so many really great business minds desperately wanting to do the same.

My thought is that we have these amazing things inside of our bodies called souls that get fed when we take the focus off of ourselves and help someone else. We truly come alive. When you get that feeling once, it feels so good you want to do it over and over again.

Our souls get fed when we help others. Some are called to feed the homeless, to raise and shelter orphans, or to build water wells, but so many that I know are called to help business owners. That is what I am called to do. I will spend the remainder of my life pursuing that cause.

I love business owners and dream that they be successful. I want to see them thrive in all areas of life, not only in business but in their marriage, in their relationships with their kids, in their health, and even in the pursuit of growing and developing personally. I call this the wheel of balance.

I was shown this diagram, and I believe in this diagram wholeheartedly. Below is a picture of what it is. It is essentially six different areas that a business owner needs to be balanced. The six areas are relationships, health, finances, personal development, spiritual, and business/passive.

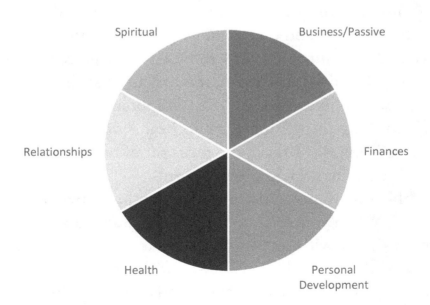

If this is a wheel, then the areas of life are the spokes on the wheel. If one of the spokes is broken, then the wheel does not roll properly. For instance, if you were about to get divorced, then the business and the other areas of your life are going to suffer. If you have a debilitating disease, then the business and the other areas are going to suffer. All the areas need to be in balance, or that's what we are striving for, at least.

Now on my wheel, there are six categories; however, you could have more, and they could be different. The crucial element though is that our lives are in balance, we feel complete, and we are not being absorbed by our own business.

Nothing is more gratifying than giving back. Giving back, paying it forward, whatever you want to call it—it is oxygen for the soul. It has the ability to cure selfishness and even depression. We live in a society and a culture that puts the focus 100 percent on the self. In this environment, it is easy to be selfish, and because happiness doesn't last, disappointment easily sets in. One of the best ways to beat disappointment and selfishness is to take the focus off of ourselves and put it on others. Help them succeed.

No one wants to reach the mountaintop by themselves. When you reach that goal, you want to take as many people with you as you can; that is what will lead to a fulfilling life. That will be a life you can be proud of. Life is all about relationships, and on our deathbeds, that is all that we will be remembered for.

First One Syndrome

I don't know if you remember how much fear you probably had in your twenties or maybe in your thirties about buying your first house. If you were like me, you had absolutely zero counsel. I had no one in my family who had ever bought a house that early. No one was telling me to race out and buy a property; in fact, they were telling me the opposite. What I heard was "What are you thinking? You are too young. You have never owned a property before. Do you even know what a mortgage is?" Those were some of the questions I heard when I was about to buy my first property.

I will be honest, I almost didn't buy it because of those thoughts. What I did know was that I had run through the numbers, and I really believed it made all the financial sense in the world.

When I bought my first house, I actually bought a three-bedroom house. My goal was that I was going to get two of my buddies to live with me, and I would charge them rent. When I ran these numbers on paper, I knew that my mortgage payment was going to be about $900 a month. I also knew that the two renters were going to pay me $450 each. So when I looked at those numbers, I knew I was going to actually pay nothing to own this home.

So I took the plunge; I bought the house. I went against what everyone was telling me. It ended up being the best financial decision I made in my twenties. The problem was that I was getting advice from people who were not qualified to give me advice. I lacked the proper mentors in my life to give me the right advice.

That is the charge you are entrusted with now: find proper advice from the people who are experienced enough to have traveled down that road. Find the guys who are well versed in and know the terrain. If you are taking advice from anyone other than that, I would argue that you are getting the wrong advice.

Now I am a man of Christian faith, and I do believe in prayerful consideration about anything you do with finances. But that also goes for just about any decision you make in life, and that is to be prayerful in that as well. I also believe, through many years of doing the opposite, that you should make sure you and your wife are in full agreement.

Like I said, I have done this many times. I went against the wishes of my wife, and so many times, it was the wrong decision. There is something unique about the intuition of women. It is this unique trait where they can know nothing about a situation, but when you fill them in on all the key components, they just seem to have a good feeling about whether it is positive or negative. It is truly amazing, as I have seen this over and over again.

CONFESSIONS OF A BANKER

Now there will be many businessmen who will probably disagree with that, and that is okay. That is just my personal belief. Regardless of that, I firmly believe in getting wise counsel before you make these huge decisions.

So I have gone over a situation I had myself when I made the decision to buy my first home. This is why I call this "the first time syndrome." It's even more pronounced when a business owner decides to buy his first building. There is this level of fear that seems to grip a large portion of business owners who are not experienced in real estate. Because of this, you will see business owners wait for many years—or for some of them, not at all—to make this decision.

The first time syndrome is very real. It's this great fear of the unknown, the fear that you have never done it before. The fear that you are making a mistake. The fear that people around you who are uneducated on the process might tell you you're making a big mistake. You will hear things like "You don't have the money for that. You don't have the expertise for that. You don't know what you're doing. You don't know where your business is going to be five years from now." The list of reasons can go on and on and on.

From my vantage point, having been in banking for fifteen years, I can tell you that the most successful business owners I know bought their own buildings. They married the two worlds of building ownership and business operations together. They took the plunge.

They found a banker who was willing to finance the property, and they figured out a way to make it happen.

The lion's share of these business owners will tell you that it was the best decision they ever made. Once they bought the building, an amazing transformation took place.

That is what this book is all about! That is why I am so passionate about seeing business owners overcome the fear, overcome the challenges of not having money to buy their own building. I tell people this all the time who want to start doing real estate deals: where there is a will, there is a way. If you want it bad enough, then you can make it happen.

I always say this in addition though: *you have got to do it the right way.* You've got to seek counsel from people with the proper education and with experience first. But once you do that and you have the desire and the fortitude, then you can/will make it happen. That is my charge to you: make it happen. I am going to help give you the counsel over the rest of these chapters. I want to help you lay out the game plan to make it happen. I hope this book inspires you to have the desire not only to learn more but to take the action necessary to make it happen.

I fully believe that once you do this right and successfully buy your own building, it will change the way you operate as a business owner. It is all about mindset. It is all about planting that seed. So let's plant that seed!

How to Finance

Once you have decided that this is a good decision for you as the business owner, how to finance this transaction is the most important part of the process. There are a couple of options you can go with.

The first and most popular option is to go down to your bank and get a commercial real estate loan. I have mentioned previously that this is the most popular loan that the bank wants to do, as it does not count against any of their loan ratio requirements with the FDIC.

Generally, they will require that you put 20%–25% down as your capital injection to the loan. This is by far the hardest problem for the majority of business owners. If you find a building for $1 million, then you as the business owner have to come up with $200,000–$250,000. For the lion's share of business owners, this is where they give up and say, "I cannot do this," and the process for them stops right there.

For me, this part of the book is the most critical part for all those individuals. I will repeat this over and over again: where there is a will, there is a way. Where there is a will, there is a way.

Business owners have to adopt this mindset when it comes to buying a building. There are other options for overcoming the down payment, and we are going to go over those.

The other main option is an SBA loan. SBA might have higher up-front fees, but they offer a really unique program that can put as little as 10% down if the building is owner-occupied. In that same scenario (the $1 million loan), that down payment would only be $100,000. SBA is also incredibly flexible, in that you can potentially add business loans inside that same building loan and get that additional money spread out over a longer amortization. For instance, let's say the business needed a $200,000 working line of credit. The SBA loan would actually be a total combined loan of $1.2 million, with the same 10% down ($120,000). Now combined, the total loan would all be at a potential twenty-five-year amortization.

Now that is a game changer for a business. That will potentially revolutionize your business, not only with the building as an asset but with the additional capital. Not only will it ensure growth, but it will also insulate against unforeseen challenges.

Now I will tell you this from experience: you have to find the right SBA lender, and those guys are very difficult to find. Our company has access to these kinds of SBA lenders.

Another type of lender is a hard money lender. The name of this lender fits the description perfectly.

They are hard. They hurt. A typical hard money lender may charge 10%–15%, with one to three points as an up-front origination.

This is a lender of last resort. In a normal situation, you do not want to use this type of lender. But if you need to close quickly and you think you have a really strong deal, then this lender could be very useful. This is why you will want to know about them and to have a couple of them in your contact list.

There is another type of lender once your transaction goes above about $7 million. This loan is called a commercial mortgage-backed security, or CMBS. Now this type of loan is very similar to mortgage-backed securities, in that they are pooled together in the form of a bond and sold on Wall Street.

This loan is strictly based on the asset only. It does not take into account the assets and financial strength of the owners. The asset/property stands alone. This is a wonderful type of loan if you can get it.

Now the deals we are talking about as a beginning commercial building owner generally do not fall into this category; therefore, I do not want to spend much time addressing it.

A couple of the main attributes of a CMBS loan is that you will get a long-term fixed rate and nonrecourse to the ownership group.

Nonrecourse is something I do want to address, because this is a very big deal as an investor. Generally, building loans will go under some type of entity name.

That could be the business name or an entity that the company sets up just to hold the property. In either scenario, the bank or lender will get the primary business owner to sign a personal guarantee.

So the loan itself will not be in the business owner's name, nor will it show up on a credit report. The business owner though will be personally responsible for that loan in the event of a loss. This will have some serious ramifications.

When banks do not get paid, they will generally sue all parties involved in the transaction. They will sue the entity who made the loan, possibly the business that is responsible for the income, and certainly the business owner, individually.

This is not an enjoyable place to be as a business owner. Lawsuits are not fun, nor are they easy or affordable. Generally, the business owner will file for bankruptcy for the business and for themselves personally, to escape the true wrath of this lawsuit. I'm not going to give any legal advice here, other than to consult an attorney in the event this happens to you as a building owner.

In summary, the two main loans that a building owner will try to get is a commercial loan or an SBA loan. A CMBS loan will only be remotely feasible with a very large commercial project, generally over $7 million. While a hard money loan might be the easiest to qualify for, it has the worst rates and fees, and it should only be used out of necessity.

Partner with Investors

I mentioned this earlier in the book, the old adage: "Where there is a will, there is a way." In this chapter, the decision to buy a building is no different. It is going to take a lot of guts and a lot of desire to make this happen. I will repeat though, where there is a will, you can make a way.

This is the number one complaint, the largest amount of resistance I encounter when I talk to small-business owners and encourage them to buy their own building. They inevitably say, *"I don't have the money."* This is always the number one reason people don't buy real estate, whether residential or commercial. It is a valid reason, no doubt. It is real.

But you *cannot* give in to that statement! You *cannot* throw in the towel and say, "Well, I will wait another five years before I start." You *cannot* let that statement, which is truth, define you, because that's not the full story!

You not having money is true, but there are so many people out there who do have money and who are looking for real estate to invest in. Let me repeat this: tons of people out there have the cash you need, and they are looking for real estate to invest in.

What these potential investors are looking for are good properties with great tenants. Guess what you have—a good property! And you're a great tenant!

In fact, you are the best tenant, because you have a vested interest in that property working out. You have a vested interest in your business continuing to work so that your real estate will continue to work. If your real estate is working, then you are making those payments year after year after year, and your equity spread in that property is rising significantly.

That, to me, is the perfect match. It is a very doable partnership. You just need to find an investor. I would care to guess that the investor you're looking for is in your current network. You just have to start asking and sharing your story.

Now investors' first question is always "What's in it for me?" They inevitably feel that the money they are bringing to the table is the most valuable piece of the equation. While I totally disagree with them, you cannot argue with them, because they have the money! The person with the money always wins. That guy generally calls the shots. No deals ever get money done without the money. Someone has to put up the money for every financial transaction that takes place in our world. We all get it, right?

My argument to them is that your side is actually the most important. You found the property, *and* you're the tenant. Or in a multiple-tenant situation, you're probably going to be the new anchor tenant. To me, you are far more valuable to the deal, but the money guy will always disagree. To prove my point, here is a fascinating story.

I know a really interesting business operator who ran/still runs an outstanding business in the kids' sports industry. He was still early in his business career, but he had already proven the success of the business model. He already had one location he had rented, and he wanted to open a second and a third location. But he didn't have the money for the down payment that the bank wanted.

Well, he did what I suggested here, and he found a partner who did have the money for the down payment. The partner thought his money for the down payment was the most important piece of this deal, but the business owner, over time, proved otherwise.

They built the second and third locations, and they proved to be a massive success. Both of the locations generated enormous profits. They were paying the building down on a fifteen-year note, and they still made several hundred thousand dollars a year.

The business group walked this scenario out five years, and in that time, tremendous appreciation in the building occurred, along with almost one-third principal reduction. Well, the investors wanted some cash out of this building because it was cash-flowing so well, and the business owner said no.

He knew who the real key to this business relationship was. It was him and his business. He told those investors to go fly a kite. After that, a lawsuit came to life, and the investors ended up losing because of their greed. After the split, the business owner was now flush with cash and did not need investors anymore.

I was the banker in this particular story, and I had a front-row seat to all the proceedings. I can tell you firsthand that the business and the business owner are more valuable, although, even in that story, I don't think the investors ever realized that. I am not sure the majority of investors ever change their minds about that.

Now that story is an extreme example of my argument, because that particular business became so successful. The majority of businesses will never be as successful as that one, but that doesn't make the statement any less true.

I wanted to reinforce that statement to get the readers out of the mindset that they bring nothing to the table. Lose that mindset. I will repeat it again: lose that mindset. You bring enormous value to the table. Always remember that. So when you negotiate with these investors for their down payment money, try to convey the value you bring to the table.

We know that the investors are looking for a good rate of return. We need to structure the deal to accommodate what they want. Now a lot of you guys reading this probably don't want investors. I get that; I don't blame you. But this is one important point that I want to convey as well: use the investors for the purchase of your first building only.

Again, the goal is to use the investor for the first property only. After you digest the first property and have paid off the property for a period of three to five years, then you can sell the building and hopefully have enough cash to buy the second building on your own.

In this scenario, the investors become a bridge for you to accomplish what your real goals are. Your goal is to have not just one building; your goal is to have multiple buildings. Now that you have sold your first building, you are armed with not only the capital but also the confidence to do that same process over again. This time though, you do not have an investor.

Structure

How are you going to structure the deal?

This is also a very important component to making a deal with an investor. Again, an investor only cares about what he's getting. He only cares about his rate of return. So you've got to make that your top priority when you're trying to sell this to him. Here are the items you have to address in determining what percentage of ownership and preferred payments you're willing to give up.

1. Does the investor have to guarantee the note? *If he does not have to guarantee the note and the*

bank approves you as the guarantor, your percentage of ownership will increase. Now you will be taking on more of the risk, but that is why you are making more money.

2. How much cash and percentage are you requiring the investor to invest as a down payment? *If you can put some money down, then you will get a larger percentage of ownership.* If you make the investor put down 100% of the required down payment by the bank, then he will expect a larger percentage. However, if the bank wants 20% as a down payment and you have 5% of the down payment, then the investor will only be putting down 15%. Then your ownership will increase, and the investor will have more confidence in the deal.

3. What percentage of a full rent payment is your business willing to pay? *If the full payment from a potential lessee is $4,000 a month and you only want to pay $2,000 a month, then your percentage ownership will be less.* If you pay the full amount, then your ownership will likely be higher. The investor may not give you a choice on this as well and may expect the full retail payment to be covered by your business.

4. Who is going to manage the building (leasing and ongoing maintenance), manage the rehab (if needed), and manage and collect the payments? *If you are going to do this, your percentage*

ownership will increase. Property management companies are generally employed for commercial buildings, but if you are taking the responsibility of those duties, then you should be able to negotiate that as payment/ownership as well.

So here are a couple of scenarios that we will run through, and we will assume the same purchase price and down payment required by the bank.

Purchase price: $1 million
Down payment required: $200,000 (20%)

A. *Investor guarantees nothing but puts a 20% down payment.* I would definitely want his ownership to be less than 50%. I would start with maybe 30% and negotiate a payback of his down payment (his 20% down payment). Then you can settle somewhere between 30% and 50% ownership. You might have a buyout clause in there. He may or may not want a guaranteed payment. It is all negotiable.

B. *Investor guarantees the loan by himself and puts a 20% down payment.* He would probably command 75% ownership or more. Because of his risk, he deserves the lion's share of ownership and profit. He is also going to negotiate for probably monthly guaranteed payments, but having 25% ownership is better than having no ownership at all. If you have no guarantee as well, then you're going to be in a good position.

C. *Investor guarantees half of the loan, and you guarantee half of the loan.* The down payment is obviously still a huge factor, but you hope that you can put down at least 5%. If you can do that, then you hope to negotiate a 40%–50% ownership stake.

As you can see, many more variables can come into play. What I want you guys to start thinking about is how these factors weigh in on your negotiations. Go into these negotiations with the mindset of the value that you and your business bring to the table. Investors want successful properties, and you need to convey how this project is going to be successful.

This is not the easiest thing to accomplish, but it can be done. So have that mindset. You are valuable, and your business is valuable. Have the mindset also that the goal is to only need this investor one time. So much of being a success in this world we live in is about having the right mindset. This particular process is no different, but do *not* give up on the dream. It can be done.

Due Diligence

This is one of the most important parts of your acquisition, and that is to make sure you properly inspect the building thoroughly. When you think of money pits for a home, a commercial building can dwarf any money pit scenario you can possibly imagine. All the costs get magnified. That is why it is so important that we do this properly.

Get plenty of inspections. Line up a roofing inspection, an HVAC inspection, a plumbing inspection, and an overall inspection of the entire building. When you have your home inspected, generally you only have to call in one inspector, but on a commercial inspection, you literally have to get all the pros in there.

The reason it is imperative is that each one of these trades will set you back an enormous amount of money. Replacing a new roof can easily be $50,000 or more. The plumbing and the HVAC can also be thousands upon thousands of dollars. So do not skimp on these inspections and make sure you do them properly.

The good part about doing a commercial transaction is that if you are dealing with another investor, you are dealing with another potential business owner.

Even though you may be dealing with ego, investors and business owners generally do not get caught up in emotion. It is just business.

So when that roof needs to be replaced and the cost is $50,000, you just renegotiate with the seller. They understand the major components, and they would be doing the same thing if they were in your shoes.

One of the unique things about a commercial property compared to a residential property is that there are different valuations involved in coming up with a price. In the residential world, it's a lot more simplistic. You simply derive your value based on the sales price of the three houses in the same subdivision and with the same square footage in your neighborhood. If your neighbor's home sold for $300,000 and your second neighbor's house sold for $310,000 and your third neighbor's house sold for $315,000, then it's very easy to extract the price of what you're going to sell yours for.

In the commercial world, it is much more difficult. There generally aren't comparable properties to yours in the close vicinity. Most commercial properties are not created equal to the next one. They vary. They vary in size; they vary in shape. The roofing structures will vary. The building materials will vary. That makes it much more difficult to decide on a value.

In summary, be very thorough in your due diligence before you close on that deal.

Success Stories

I'm hoping that this chapter will be very powerful for all you guys who have made it this far into the book. This book was written for the average, everyday business owner out there, wondering how to increase his/her bottom line and how to run a business better. I have always believed—and still believe—that adding commercial real estate to a business owner's portfolio is one of the best things they can do financially. Over time, this creates not only net worth but also potentially sustainable cash flow monthly.

So the business owners I'm going to speak of are *real* business owners I know, and I have had the privilege of financing a portion of the buildings that they own and that I am going to write about. They are just average, everyday guys who bought a building for their business and over time bought additional real estate, and all of them have a net worth in excess of $1 million. There are no Warren Buffetts, no Elon Musks, no hedge fund managers, and no private equity guys here, just inspiring business owners who worked hard and persevered, who I personally know.

They lived through exactly what I have talked about in this book. They struggled with acquiring the first one, but once that was digested and stabilized, they bought subsequent buildings. I am going to go over, on a summary level, how each one evolved from the first building to the last, being the present day.

I hope this will inspire you and show you that it can be done and that you should always have the mindset of "How do I make this happen?" instead of the opposite, which is "I can't do it because of this, this, and this."

The age makeup of these guys ranges from thirty-five to sixty-five years old, and I can tell you that none of them are done with their investing careers. They will be at this game until they turn in their knives and forks.

Number 1 starts a solo CPA practice. One of his clients has a hotel. He becomes good friends with him and invests a considerable amount of money for a hotel deal. That builder doesn't honor his commitment, and the CPA has to step in and figure out how to build a hotel. He does not have expertise in building a hotel, but he finds the proper individuals to help. They get it completed.

A couple of years go by, and this hotel is sold, without a lot of money made. But the investor has been born inside of him. His confidence has grown, and he then proceeds to build a second hotel. This time, he becomes the builder/developer and majority owner.

This goes well, and within a couple of years, the equity position in this second hotel is substantial.

He sells this second hotel as well, although this time he has over a million dollars from the proceeds. With this influx of capital, he builds a third hotel, brimming with experience and confidence not only in himself but in the banks as well.

This third hotel is another success, and because he is the general contractor/builder, his savings from the development and build is around 15%–20%. For easy math, let's say it's a $5 million build. The general contractor would have charged $750,000 to $1 million for the build. He saves that amount because he does it himself. The bank makes him pay $1.25 million down payment (25%) and finances $3.75 million.

A couple of years go by, and he takes a cash out refinance loan and pulls his entire down payment from the third hotel, essentially having no cash out of pocket from that hotel. Let's say the new loans appraisal is $7.5 million, a $2.5 million increase. The bank allows a 70% cash-out of the $7.5 million appraisal, a loan amount of $5.25 million. He now has cash proceeds of $5.25 million minus $3.6 million (now owed), which is $1.65 million. He puts $1.25 million down on the original loan and now gets back $1.65 million. He has no money out of pocket and now has $400,000 additional.

With the cash proceeds, he builds his fourth hotel, a second one to own and keep, with largely similar numbers to the previous example. Let's say it's a $5.5 million build, and the bank asks for 25% down payment again. This time, the down payment is $1.375 million, which he has from the cash-out refinance.

He then repeats the same process. A couple of years later, he does a cash-out refinance with the increase in equity similar to the above. Now he owns two hotels, and none of his own money is invested in them. He owes about $5 million to $5.5 million on two hotels that are worth around $7.5 million each, so his equity in the two hotels is around $5 million as well.

I didn't even mention that each hotel is kicking off cash flow of about $250,000–$450,000 each because he is a great operator. At this point, any bank around will finance his further expansion, and he is absolutely enjoying life.

You can see from the example the evolution of this individual. He went from getting screwed over by his investor/builder friend to getting thrown into the deep end of the pool. He was frightened when he was abandoned by his friend. What was his response though? He rolled up his sleeves and learned and embraced the opportunity. He took something that would have bankrupted and mentally destroyed most individuals, and he made it a positive. He took that experience and decided to build another hotel—only this time, he'd do it properly. I absolutely love this story and this guy's mindset and mental toughness. That's tough.

CONFESSIONS OF A BANKER

Well, fast-forward another five or so years, and this same guy has done that process two more times for a total of four hotels owned, all with similar numbers. His equity is approaching $10 million, and he has a fifth hotel in the works. Brilliant.

Number 2 drops out of college to start a business. He is a revolutionary. He is on the cutting edge of an industry that is in its infancy. He is a pioneer, almost by accident. The industry is discount overstock merchandise; think TJ Maxx. He sells to these guys.

He is going to a college town and sees a business going out of business. He enters the store and talks to the owner; the owner is trying to liquidate the entire store, which is a men's clothing store. He is only interested in acquiring some of the furniture. The owner tries to sell him everything and throws in the furniture. He bites.

His parents had owned a business as well, so he thinks he can liquidate the clothing without too much fear. He ends up doing much better than he ever imagined, and the entrepreneur is born. He proceeds to partner with his cousin, duplicates that process many times over, moves to a metropolitan area, and becomes very successful. He knows that at some point, he has to buy a building.

About four years into the business, he stumbles on a deal where the owner wants to sell the merchandise but has a small building listed for sale as well. Not only do they buy the merchandise, but they negotiate for the building as well. The offer is for owner financing, meaning that the owner/seller, not a bank, will carry the note for a sizable down payment.

This building is a warehouse. The price is roughly $500,000, and they have to come up with a $75,000 down payment. They borrow some from family, but they know the merchandise they just bought will fetch a premium and pay back a large chunk of the down payment. You can imagine how this story turns out. They are right; the merchandise sells at a huge premium and makes back a lion's share of the down payment.

They proceed to move the business into the building and operate out of the building for about five years. They start to outgrow the building and decide it's time to move out and up. They find a bigger building and put this building up for sale. The building sells for something like $850,000 at a sizable profit, but the cash proceeds are significant. They probably owed about $350,000, and they net about $500,000 in cash upon the sale.

Now armed with the knowledge of the warehouse space, they buy a bigger building, but it's a building in need of repair. In the commercial world, this type of acquisition would be called a value add. The premise is that the owner will rehab the building, thereby obtaining a higher-quality tenant at a higher rate, which will also increase the valuation. In this case, the tenant is themselves, which is why this strategy makes so much sense.

CONFESSIONS OF A BANKER

The math on this building looks something like this: a price of $1.1 million and an earmarked $250,000 for rehab. In the bank's eyes, they add those numbers together and want 20% down ($1.35 million multiplied by 20%, so $270,000 down payment) and a loan amount of $1.08 million. They have the entire down payment amount from the proceeds from the previous sale. Now the business moves into the new building and is the tenant, which, by the way, is the best tenant you can have.

A couple of years go by, and they sell the building in the neighborhood of $1.9 million to another company that wants to occupy the building. The net proceeds are something like $900,000 after closing costs.

Then they buy another building, selling out and trading up again. This time, the building is much bigger, but they do another value add transaction. The building is $1.8 million and needs about $400,000, for a total cost basis of $2.2 million. The down payment is 20%, about $440,000. They easily have that amount from the previous sale and still have $460,000 in the bank.

Once again, they move their business into the property. This time though, they decide to keep the property and find a tenant to replace them, with the intent to buy another building. On a value-add play, the one drawback is that it can take a considerable amount of time to find a tenant. They plan on having a vacant building for a period of twelve to eighteen months. In their case though, the business rents the entire time. It's a beautiful scenario, and it can be incredibly effective.

They find a tenant and do a long-term lease on an NNN basis, which is going to command the highest sales price. Their logic is that they want to enjoy the cash flow for a period of about two years and then sell. It's another beautiful strategy that works to perfection.

In the meantime, they find another vacant building for just about the same type of numbers and have that down payment as well from the prior sale. So at this point, they have two buildings. One is on an NNN lease with a really good lease rate, and the other is a new building they have moved their business into and are doing rehab to.

Roughly two years go by, and they sell the third building to an investor for roughly $2.8 million. The profit is $600,000, but with the two years of payments, another $100,000 has been knocked off the note with the bank. The amount owed is close to $1.55 million, and they receive net proceeds of $1.25 million and still own the fourth building.

They do the same strategy two more times, with similar results. You can see that in this scenario as well, millions have been created in long-term wealth for this entrepreneur. His evolution has led him to become so skilled at the warehouse value-add play that he has become an expert in the niche. He eventually sells his business to his partner, and he focuses solely on commercial real estate.

CONFESSIONS OF A BANKER

Number 3 is an attorney. Just like the others, he almost stumbles into his first building and thinks nothing of it because it seems so insignificant. He starts his own practice and works sixty to eighty hours a week. He devotes himself to the grind of building his practice. He takes great pride in his practice. A couple of years in, he has been renting a building for a while and somehow stumbles into a conversation with a friend that goes something like this: "Why don't you buy my building? It's perfect for your law firm. It's the right amount of space, and I'll give you a great deal." The property is a residential house that just happens to be in a neighborhood on a busy street wherein the city changed the zoning to commercial. That, in most cases, raises the property value of the former house.

In this case, the price is something like $130,000. The owner even carries the note for the attorney with 10% down. The attorney moves his practice into the house and carries on with his business, paying less than what he used to be paying in rent.

A couple of years later, he wants to expand his practice to another part of the metroplex. This time, he embraces the thought of buying a second building instead of renting. He buys a building for something like $200,000 and starts his second practice. He decides that the location is not a right fit for the business and looks to sell that building and buy another one closer to his home.

He sells the building for, let's say, $275,000, profiting $75,000, and finds another one on a major freeway. He buys the building for $375,000, and the bank wants 20%, which is $75,000, the exact amount of profit from the other building. He consolidates both practices back into this one location and rents out the small house, which easily covers the note and generates cash flow.

Several years go by, and he decides he is ready for a much larger practice. He decides to keep the building on the major freeway, buy a larger building closer to the downtown area, and have two practices again. This time, the building is a multitenant building. These are great buildings, as you can rent out the additional square footage, and then all or a large portion of your rent is covered by the additional tenants. He loves this model.

A few more years go by, and the building he bought for $375,000 on the freeway gets some unexpected great news. The freeway is going to be expanded, and this stretch of the freeway gets bought by the department of transportation (DOT).

A few months pass as negotiations go back and forth, and he settles with the DOT for about $450,000 for taking a portion of his parking lot. They grandfather his smaller parking lot so that it will still be up to the city's zoning code. So at this point, he has a negative cost basis on the building. The bank allows him to keep all the money from the DOT because when

CONFESSIONS OF A BANKER

they reappraise the building, they find that he has substantial equity in it. The building is still appraised for $550,000 after the reduction in parking spots. At this point, he still owes about $225,000, but he gets to keep all of the $450,000 in what is one of the greatest scenarios I have personally been involved in.

The bigger multitenant building he has bought is around $900,000 and needs about $200,000 in rehab, for a total cost of $1.1 million. The bank again wants 20% down, $220,000, which he easily covers, and the lion's share of his debt service is covered by the additional tenants. This is one of my favorite strategies, by the way. You buy more of a building than you need, but the goal is to have *all* or at least a large portion of the total payment covered by tenants.

You know how this story goes by now. Several years go by, and the property continues to appreciate. He comes across a whale of a property that is priced at an absolute steal. It's a huge property, which causes quite a bit of anxiety, along with a massive amount of due diligence.

It is a twelve-story high-rise downtown. The seller has a cost basis of $7.5 million and had at one point tried to sell the property for over $10 million, but 2008 happened. His occupancy had fallen substantially, and so had his interest in being a good property manager. The building is in disarray. His price is $4 million. It is loaded with risks, but the lawyer calculates all those into his strategy and buys the property. The bank wants a massive 20% down payment, 800,000; however, his law firm has had a few record years, and he has the money set aside for the purchase.

He also decides to sell the previous multitenant building, and he scores big on that sale. He sells the building for $1.7 million and cashes out net proceeds of around $900,000 after the close, which more than covers the twelve-story high-rise.

The twelve-story high-rise obviously needs work through the years, but the occupancy has grown to over 80%. He is able to do the repairs in small doses as the years progress, mostly from his cash flow. It's a beautiful strategy, and currently, he still owns the building. The estimate of the current value is close to $12 million. He probably has over $9 million in equity.

Number 4 is the sports gym operator from the previous chapter. This particular business owner is in the kids' sports space. In the area we live, that has become big business. He and his wife are one of the first to be on the entry point of that segment. His first gym, he, of course, rents. He runs a great operation. He is meticulous about how his gym is run from the operational standpoint. Naturally, he has success and opens a second gym, which he also rents. That gym becomes very profitable.

His dream is to have multiple facilities, but the real net worth is about to start. For the third facility, he seeks investors and partners with a couple of them, and they build their own building. What they do is bril-

CONFESSIONS OF A BANKER

liant. They buy excess land and build their building in the back, which does not have frontage from the highway.

Their business becomes a destination, meaning that these parents would find them. The purpose is to build a road right in between the land so that you have two rectangles of raw dirt, zoned commercial, that you can sell off individually. Here is the breakdown of the numbers: the land is purchased for a total of $1.1 million. The building cost is around $2.8 million, for a total of $3.9 million.

As soon as the road is cut in for their building that now sits in the back, they put the two parcels of land up for sale. The first one is sold immediately to a dental group for $900,000. The other one takes a little bit of time, but it is also sold for around $900,000. The genius in that is that the land is now not only free, but the profit on the land is $700,000, which now reduces the cost basis of the total project. The cost basis now becomes $2.1 million for a building that is worth around $3.7 million.

Almost as soon as that project is started, the same investors agree to start a second facility as well in another town. So this is the fourth facility that the business owner is going to run, but the second facility that he is going to own. He and the investors do a fifty-fifty split on both of the buildings.

Both of the buildings end up being a massive success, and all the parties enjoy the fruits of that. The second facility that was built did not have the luxury of additional land. The numbers on that were something like $600,000 for the land and the same $2.8 million for the building. Because the cash flow from the operations is so strong, both of the buildings are put on fifteen-year notes.

There are pros and cons to a fifteen-year note, as you can imagine. The pro is that you have a massive amount of money that goes to principal each month. Also, fifteen years in the commercial real estate world go by really fast, and more times than not, you will see property appreciate 70%–125% regularly. The combination creates a massive net worth.

The con obviously is that the payment is much higher, which can constrict cash flows. So you only want to do a fifteen-year note if the cash flow is going to be really strong. For this particular business owner, almost every facility he opens enjoys strong cash flows.

About three years after digesting those two, the business owner builds another facility—only this time, he does not need the investors. He is able to put down the 20% down payment on his own. The numbers are again very similar to the two we have already described above.

This happens again and again and again. I won't bore you with the details of each of the three, but they are similar in each instance. At this point, the business owner has six facilities that he owns, with so much equity in each one.

Another detail I left out was that prior to building even the first one, the business owner had the foresight to hire a friend of his to be an in-house builder. The reason was very clever: the build-out of these facilities, whether they leased a facility or built a new one, was that they needed a general contractor (GC) on either. Instead of using a GC individually, the numbers made more sense to have one on staff full-time. Consequently, the building cost of around $2.8 million came with about 15% GC savings. So each building would have cost in excess of an additional $400,000. You can see why it was cheaper to just have a builder on staff.

At this point, a much bigger bank comes in to play and refinances all six of the properties, including enough money to buy out the investors from the first two facilities. At this point, if the business owner were to stop, which he does not intend to, and just get the properties paid off (through existing cash flow of the business), the six buildings, at an average of $4 million each, would be a net worth of $24 million.

This is one of the best examples you'll ever find with the perfect synergy between a business and real estate. That is, you create a business that you can duplicate over and over, but you become the best tenant for the building. Then you build facility after facility after facility.

Number 5 is a jewelry store owner. All these stories have the first key question of "How did you get the first one?" We know how the business owner/investor got the second building, the third building, the tenth building. The question is always "How did you get the first?" The last business owner I am going to talk about has a unique story, just like all the rest. He and his brother grew up with parents who were in the pawn-shop business. They were well groomed in the art of buying low and selling high. That alone is an incredible skill to possess.

This business owner and his brother start a jewelry store together. They rent a location, partner up, then run the store together for several years. Ultimately, they decide to go their separate ways. This business owner decides to open his own jewelry store. He has always wanted to own his own building, but just like it is for most people, the down payment is a bit of a challenge.

When he looks for the building to open his jewelry store, he intentionally looks for a building that will allow him the option to purchase it at a later date. He has incredible foresight in negotiating this into the contract. He operates the jewelry store for a few years, and he comes to me to finance the building. He has been very successful with his new store, and we are happy to oblige.

Earlier, I talked about the attorney buying a building that was taken by the department of transportation. This business owner also has his building on the same freeway. Just like the attorney, the DOT takes a large portion of his parking lot. In his case, they also take a portion of his building. In the same instance,

CONFESSIONS OF A BANKER

after several rounds of negotiation between their attorneys, the DOT ends up paying for his building. This covers 100% of his purchase price and renovations, so he essentially gets the building for free. The number is somewhere around $375,000. He also gets to keep every bit of those proceeds, as his building still has enough value for the loan.

After a few years, he is ready to open a second store. In this instance, he also negotiates on a lease that gives him the option to buy the building at a later date. The purchase price for this building is around $500,000. This particular building does not necessarily have any equity in it, but it is exactly what he needs to operate his business. He is willing to pay full price for the option of buying the building. This gives him several years to decide if this location is going to be a profitable one or not. His thinking is, if it is not profitable, then he will finish up the lease and not buy the building and potentially move to another location.

This location also becomes a winner, and he decides to purchase the building. The bank requires 20% down, and he has more than enough. Armed with confidence and knowledge, he starts to pursue more commercial real estate.

For his third building, he finds an old restaurant on a major thoroughfare for cheap. This is bought after 2008 but right before everything starts to appreciate, so he buys it at a low. The number on this building is around $250,000. This particular business owner does not like debt at all and always prefers to pay cash. In this case, he pays for this building in cash. About three to four years later, he gets an offer on the building for almost $675,000, and he accepts the offer.

Earlier, in the description of this individual, I referenced that he had learned how to buy low and sell high at an early age, and this skill obviously carried over into real estate. Before he sells the third building, he purchases a primary residence out of foreclosure for around $700,000, and within five years, he sells this as well for around $1.1 million. He was able to enjoy the splendor of this house for many years and then still profit handsomely from that sale. That is also part of the fun of learning this art. You get to enjoy these buildings while you are paying down the note and enjoying appreciation.

Also, during that same period, he buys another building for $875,000. His purchase of this building is based on pure speculation that one day he might open his third jewelry store. The price is higher than he would like, but it is in a very high rent district. At the time of writing, he still owns this building.

As I have written about these five individuals, again, each one of these business owners I personally know, and I financed the majority of these properties. The reason I went to such great lengths to detail each person's transactions was to, again, show everyone reading this book that this is possible. It's not just possible; it is the evolution you will partake in. Your knowledge,

CONFESSIONS OF A BANKER

your acumen, your confidence, and your wherewithal will all grow significantly as you go through this process. This is not just some kind of motivational monologue; it is what I see over and over and over again with business owners who decide to buy their own building. My hope is that you guys will just decide that you can and that you will do this. You will not let anyone tell you that you cannot. Shift your mindset to one that embraces this dream. Do not settle for less.

I wish you all the best of luck in your new endeavor.

About the Author

Shane Mara has been a banker for fifteen-plus years and a real estate investor for twenty-plus years, and he calls on that experience and the experience of working alongside some of the very best small-business owners for this message. He is passionate about blending these two worlds together. His desire is to see business owners excel and not struggle, to see them build wealth and not be undone by stress and worry from struggling with business.

Printed in the USA
CPSIA information can be obtained
at www.ICGtesting.com
LVHW041520140924
790863LV00003B/478